Values, Vision, and Versatility

Values, Vision, and Versatility

The True Power of the Trio

COREY HICKS

VALUES, VISION, AND VERSATILITY
THE TRUE POWER OF THE TRIO

Design and artwork for the book: Cyril Etienne, Etienne Creations. Lakeland Florida

iUniverse books may be ordered through booksellers or by contacting:

iUniverse
1663 Liberty Drive
Bloomington, IN 47403
www.iuniverse.com
1-800-Authors (1-800-288-4677)

ISBN: 978-1-4917-8220-0 (sc)
ISBN: 978-1-4917-8218-7 (hc)
ISBN: 978-1-4917-8219-4 (e)

Library of Congress Control Number: 2015918079

Print information available on the last page.

iUniverse rev. date: 08/12/2016

Prologue

Values, Vision, and Versatility is an inspirational book that focuses on the three fundamental concepts that play an integral part in defining, developing, and maximizing an individual to be the best he or she can possibly be. This book answers many questions and helps uncover the passion for greatness within each of us.

Why a trio? First of all, a threefold cord is not quickly broken. Many of life's greatest and most profitable elements were discovered, explored, and produced in groups of three.

Famous Three-Word Sayings:
"Life is awesome."
"Do your best."
"Never give up."
"Success is yours."
"Keep your cool."
"Live your potential."

"My mind rules."

"Seize the day."

"Believe you can."

"Be the change."

"Action gives results."

"Do it now."

"Dare to win."

Famous Quotes about Trios:

"It takes two pieces of evidence to create a reasonable doubt, but the *third* piece changes the mind." (Unknown)

"All mankind is divided into *three* classes: Those that are immovable, those that are movable, and those that move." (Arabian Proverb)

"You have brains in your head. You have feet in your shoes. You can steer yourself any direction you choose." (Dr. Seuss)

"Today you are you.
That is truer than truehere is no one alive who is you-er than you." (Dr. Seuss)

"These *three* are the ingredients of the good life: Learning, earning, and yearning!" (Christopher Moseley)

"Turn yourself not away from *three* best things: Good Thought, Good Word, and Good Deed!" (Zoroaster)

As one can see, the concept of three is not a novel or a new concept; it is a powerful force that produces an element to be reckoned with.

The word *element* is defined in *Webster's Dictionary* as "the state or sphere natural or suited to a person or thing." Element can also apply to any such part that connotes irreducible simplicity; it is any part or quality of a thing reduced to its simplest and most basic form.

Franz Kafka said, "In theory there is a possibility of perfect happiness: to believe in the indestructible element within one, and not to strive towards it."

I define *element* as a natural ability or an innate gift; with this element comes a deep, passionate desire to perform whatever gift, talent, or ability is found naturally within. In *The Element*, creativity expert Ken Robinson points out that *element* is the point where natural talent meets personal passion; he illustrates how everyone can find one's element and connect with one's true talents and fulfill one's creative potential:

An individual demonstrates his or her element as a natural gift or talent; it is what he or she is supernaturally meant to perform. One could even say it is this "supernatural element" that defines who we are as individuals and resonates within us as an illuminating glow. The element helps us bare the deepest secrets and desires of our heart that are truly fueled by passion.

One expresses one's element when one—against all odds, opposition, and objections—excels in the vocation, occupation, calling, or talent deeply embedded within. Continuing in that element—come rain or shine, encouragement or discouragement, strength or weakness—moves one toward one's intended purpose. When one works within this element, one experiences a euphoric burst that brings clarity to mind and body.

Throughout life, there are many stages one must emerge from in order to have an ultimate understanding of one's personal element. Each stage builds character and teaches patience in one's quest for definition and completion.

Several self-help resources offer simple surveys that help one determine what one is meant to be or do. Determining one's element may be as simple as answering some questions. What is your best quality? How would your friends and colleagues describe you? What do you like to do on weekends? How would you like to spend your evenings? What epiphany has occurred that brought you to a point of self-exploration?

Answering these simple questions and discovering one's specific supernatural element serves as an internal homeostasis that regulates one's subconscious and brings about internal happiness; happiness releases endorphins that ultimately produce peace in the soul.

When one works within this supernatural element, one's soul will be at peace and that peace will bring contentment to the heart; one will find favor in any task as a direct result. One may not be aware that the Trio—values, vision, and versatility—is working within.

I have come to the conclusion that life becomes a journey of purposeful meaning when one begins to understand the power of element. This supernatural element is built upon love; if implemented, it serves as a blueprint for happiness. Life takes each of us on a journey to discover and uncover happiness and joy through this element.

Creativity expert Ken Robinson believes that we are all born with tremendous natural capacities, but we lose touch with them as we spend more time in the world. Many people are not aware of what they are really capable of achieving, whether it's a child feeling bored in class, an employee being misused, or even someone who feels frustrated and can't explain why.

Education, business, and society are losing out. *The Element* draws on the stories of a wide range of people— from ex-Beatles member Paul McCartney to renowned physicist Richard Feynman and many business leaders and athletes—showing how all of them came to recognize their unique talents and were able to make a successful living doing what they love.

As I think back on my own experience with my parents, I can't help but reflect on what caused me to search for and realize my purpose, destiny, and element.

When searching for one's own element, ask, "What epiphany has occurred that has brought me to a point of self-exploration?"

Dictionary.com describes an epiphany as "a sudden, intuitive perception of or insight into the reality or essential meaning of something, usually initiated by some simple, homely, or commonplace occurrence or experience."

It is a sudden manifestation of the essence or meaning of something. My commonplace occurrence or experience occurred as a child—after an event that could have turned out to be a fatal experience. My epiphany helped me realize God's greater plan and purpose for my life.

One Sunday afternoon, I stayed at home while my mother attended church service. Little did I know that this would be the day that would determine how I live the rest of my life. While my father was asleep in the other room, I started an experiment that marked the first sign of God's undeniable intervention and favor; it showed me that he had predestined my purpose in life. It was my epiphany.

I had always been intrigued by electronics; it excited me and piqued my interest and curiosity. This particular Sunday I went into the bathroom of our old house—that had no circuit breaker—and closed the door behind me. I looked through the drawers for something to experiment with. I found a light bulb and an extension cord with the end severed—the electrical wiring was exposed. I decided to experiment with the electrical cord, water, and a light bulb—this was a disaster waiting to happen.

In my first experiment, I plugged the extension cord into the electrical outlet. Then, I placed the exposed, uncovered wires on each side of the base of the light bulb to see if the bulb would light up. When I realized that the bulb had either blown out or malfunctioned, I grew bored with my first experiment.

Next, I decided to experiment with electricity and water. When the sink filled, I burst with excitement and anticipation as I reached over and plugged in the extension cord; at the same time, I placed the light bulb in the palm of my hand with the exposed wires surrounding the base of the bulb.

Once the water reached its level, I shut it off. I slowly submerged my hand in the water. The current was slow but aggressive as it electrocuted me. I squeezed the base of the bulb tighter with every jolt of electrical current, but somehow, I was protected. Although I was not a science major (nor have I been since), I concluded that the moisture from my hand served as a seal around the exposed wire and ultimately stopped my fatal electrocution.

Twice I dipped my hand in and out of the water when a strange euphoria overcame me. My heartbeat felt faint, but I felt an urge to experience the feeling again. On the last try, my body grew weak and I felt as though the end was near. I had just enough energy to dispose of the evidence from my experiment and find my way to the couch. I recovered by sleeping away my injury.

I awoke from my rest determined to never to share this story, but then God gave me my revelation; I realized his intention for me was bigger than my comprehension. That was my epiphany—the sudden manifestation of the essence or meaning of my life, my purpose, and the plan God had for me. He had ordained and commissioned me to utilize the power of my testimony of undeniable favor to impact the world.

In *Science of the Soul,* Corrine McLaughlin spoke of man's essence and true identity. She said, "For the soul embodies not just loving compassion, but also purposeful will and wise intelligence. Balanced love, light, and will are the signatures of the soul."

The individual is drawn to a light or glow that produces an unexplainable attraction to his or her attainable purpose in the world.

Notes

Notes

Notes

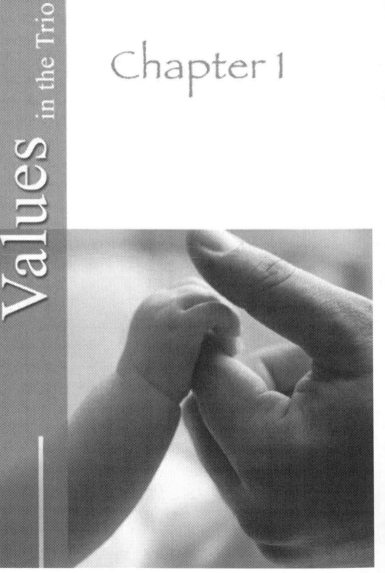

What are the **Values** in the Trio

Chapter 1

Chapter 1

The Values in the Trio

"A value is a belief, a mission, or a philosophy that is meaningful. Whether we are consciously aware of them or not, every individual has a core set of personal values. Values can range from the commonplace, such as the belief in hard work and punctuality, to the more psychological, such as self-reliance, concern for others, and harmony of purpose."

—Roy Posner

"Values are those things that really matter to each of us ... the ideas and beliefs we hold as special. Caring for others, for example, is a value; so is the freedom to express our opinions. Most of us

learned our values—or morals, if you prefer—
at home, at church or synagogue, at school."

—Lewis Orans

Values within the Trio are the good inside you that are instilled from birth. It is the self-revealing, self-sacrificing commitment to a higher, more perfect way of life; it is good to one's self and to others because it produces an unexplainable attraction.

Values, or the lack thereof, are a rare and powerful source that can unify or bring down nations. Values are the core essence of unity between the Alpha and the Omega of the internal being. In other words, it is the start and finish of whom one is. With values, one can go far, but without values, one will be diminished, devalued, and ultimately dissolved.

There have been many great individuals with phenomenal vision and versatility, but because of their lack of values, their talents were limited. Just think of some of our former greats in boxing, sports casting, politics, and entertainment. They were elevated and put in places where their character could not keep them. The primary reason was their lack of values.

When uncovering and discovering one's element, it is vital that one adhere to values that will promote the common good; it preserves you and the ones around you. Many times, when we discover this element, we are not able to sustain its power and authority because we lack implementation of the Trio in our daily lives.

Values are slowly diminishing in modern society; it has taken a backseat to mediocrity and compromise. The values of our great country have whittled away to idealistic secularism, which has brought into play the adage, "Each generation will be wiser, but yet weaker."

We must maintain our values so that we can maintain our strength; we must do this so that we are not at a stagnant holding point. If we become stagnant, we will create a void that no earthly possession will be able to fill. We will fall from the strength of the original supernatural element.

Has society begun to overlook our fundamental core principles of values, vision, and versatility—the Trio that was built from the Word of God?

Values are the key to dispelling myths, eradicating half-truths, and quieting naysayers. Values can heal a nation ruled by hatred and greed; they serve as the common denominator of hope to answer the plaguing questions of economic despair, moral decay, and worldwide ills.

Values embrace the good and are the primary arterial source to the survival of the Trio in one's life.

The two main values instilled in me from birth are perseverance and determination. The core essence of the man I am today was strategically and deeply rooted in me by my parent's values; they were two loving, hardworking people who exemplified the worth of a good. Among the many exceptional values they instilled, one particular saying comes to mind, "Anything worth having is worth working for."

My parents exemplified unbiased love and value in life. My mother and father always displayed love—whether you were a guest or a relative, a person at our house was always treated with the utmost respect and welcomed as one of the immediate family.

Although my mother had several bouts with breast cancer, she remained the major support system for our family. Despite days that were not always sunny, my mother continued as the anchor of support for her husband and her children. She continued to offer support and words of encouragement that shaped and molded the element within me. She persevered so that she could have a successful family. She was an example of sacrificial love and perseverance.

My father exemplified determination; he instilled this value in me with his endless talents and unwillingness to settle for mediocrity. My father worked on projects for countless hours and was never satisfied until the work was completed properly. He said, "Do things right the first time so you don't have to go back a second time." It is amazing how, subconsciously, this refined value is implanted within me. It surfaces at special, appropriate moments that bring me a deep appreciation for my parents.

Notes

Notes

Notes

Notes

Chapter 2

What is the Vision in the Trio

Chapter 2

The Vision in the Trio

The second segment of the Trio is vision. This segment plays a significant role because it illustrates the significance of the power of visualizing one's own potential for greatness.

Dr. Edward Watke Jr. defines *vision* as "divine perspective, divine wisdom, divine insight, and illumination." It has been said that vision is getting on your heart what God has on his.

Vision plays a significant part in the Trio because it clarifies one's true purpose and sheds light on an individual's internal element. This internal element starts with core values that ultimately help realize a person's vision.

Dictionary.com defines *vision* as "the act or power of anticipating that which will or may come to be: prophetic vision; the vision of an entrepreneur.

3. an experience in which a personage, thing, or event appears vividly or credibly to the mind, although not actually present, often under the influence of a divine or other agency: a heavenly messenger appearing in a vision.

4. something seen or otherwise perceived during such an experience: The vision revealed its message.

5. a vivid, imaginative conception or anticipation: visions of wealth and glory."

Observe what many well-known individuals have had to say about vision:

"The man doesn't make the vision; the vision makes the man."
—Pastor Yonggi Cho

Many times, the vision segment of the Trio is one of the most complicated parts due to one's lack of understanding of its power. Oftentimes, individuals are manipulated into thinking that another person's element is his or her own.

"Dissatisfaction and discouragement are not caused by the absence of things but the absence of vision."
—Anonymous

There are several publications and websites to help you establish and realize your vision. Susan Heathfield wrote an article entitled "Achieve Your Dreams: Six Steps to Accomplish Your Goals and Resolutions", which focused on these six steps:

1) You must deeply desire the goal or resolution.

2) Visualize yourself achieving your goal.

3) Make a plan for the path you need to take to achieve the goal.

4) Commit to achieving the goal by writing it down.

5) Establish times for checking your progress on the calendar.

6) Review your overall progress regularly.

"So many of our dreams seem impossible, then improbable, then inevitable."
—Christopher Reeve

There may have been times when close friends, family, or associates approached you with an idea that, in their minds, seemed to be the perfect opportunity for you. After speaking with them—convinced by their passion and excitement—you begin to put time and energy into an opportunity that does not complement the true strengths within your element.

"A vision is not just a picture of what could be; it is an appeal to our better selves, a call to become something more."
—Rosabeth Moss Kanter

One's vision and decisions will always agree with God's plan before it materializes. Dawson Trotman said, "Vision is getting on your heart what God has on His." Do not try to realize another man's vision for you—try to realize God's vision *of* you. Agreement with God always makes the vision easy to accomplish and makes doubt nonexistent.

"Where there is no vision, the people perish."
—Proverbs 29:18

"For leaders, a vision is not a dream; it is a reality that has yet to come into existence. Vision is palpable to leaders; their confidence in and dedication to vision are so strong they can devote long hours over many years to bring it into being. In this way, a vision acts as a force within, compelling a leader to action. It gives a leader purpose, and the power of the vision and the leader's devotion to it work to inspire others—who, sensing purpose and commitment, respond." —Neil Snyder and Michelle Graves, "Leadership and Vision: Importance of Goals and Objectives in Leadership"

"Vision is the art of seeing the invisible."
—Jonathan Swift

How many times has one found oneself in a situation that sounded like a great opportunity because one's thirst for capital gain overruled ones true desires of the heart? At times, we are taken on a journey that appears great, but it does not necessarily agree with our internal elements. The energy surrounding these ideas is short-lived because it creates a void. The quest for self-fulfillment lives on. After time and money have been sacrificed, the quest for self-fulfillment lives on; we continue our pursuit of happiness through self-gratification.

"Vision without a task is only a dream. A task without a vision is but drudgery. But vision with a task is a dream fulfilled."
—Anonymous

I have come to realize that vision is discovered as a result of obedience to the principles of core values. These values serve as a supernatural magnet that plays a significant role in shaping, molding, and directing the future you.

"All men dream: but not equally. Those who dream by night in the dusty recesses of their minds wake in the day to find that it was vanity: but the dreamers of the day are dangerous men, for they may act their dream with open eyes to make it possible."
—T. E. Lawrence

Many of us are trapped in a holding pattern because we neglect an important part of the Trio: vision. This negligence temporarily suspends any good that may come to the individual through the light of attraction. This light or illumination is desperately needed for vision: to solidify what God's goals are for the person. When a person follows this light, there is peace in the soul for he or she has allowed the internal lighthouse to guide him or her in the right direction.

"A leader has the vision and conviction that a dream can be achieved. He inspires the power and energy to get it done."
—Ralph Lauren

It is amazing how missing one element from the Trio significantly alters the internal element and leaves an unexplainable void. My purpose or discovery of my element was obvious, but I never had a clear sense of direction. I struggled countless times with what I assumed to be my sense of purpose. I realized the internal element—reserved by God—stimulated my mind toward my higher purpose; I could not do it on my own—I had to depend totally on God to reveal it to me.

"The vision that you glorify in your mind, the ideal that you enthrone in your heart, this you will build your life by, and this you will become."
—Anonymous

How many times has one's subconscious interceded at the right time and brought forth a moment of clarity that served as a safeguard? This visualization or favorable foresight preserves your life—and the memory of the experience is never forgotten.

"Determine that the thing can and shall be done and then we shall find the way."
—Abraham Lincoln

True vision—ability inspired by and strengthened by God—encompasses life, laughter, and love. These attributes play a significant part in the creation of visual manifestation. Visual manifestation is defined as seeing oneself in the moment. This is why the vision segment within the Trio is so important. Before one can accomplish any feat that he or she has visualized, one must first see oneself in the moment of accomplishment.

"Dream lofty dreams, and as you dream, so shall you become. Your vision is the promise of what you shall one day be. Your ideal is the prophecy of what you shall at last unveil."
—James Allen

We must always remember that just because we cannot see something does not mean that it does not exist. The true test of sight depends on your faith. In life, we find ourselves in a three-part process that involves being justified, certified, and elevated.

The vision segment of the Trio serves as the gold standard in terms of everyday struggles. No matter what we do for a career, relationship, education, or adventure, there is always a justification process that takes place to test our dedication, desire, and commitment. This process can be discouraging because challenges create an emotional roller coaster. There are many highs and lows, but anything worth having is worth working for.

During the certification stage, a deep appreciation and newfound love is established and solidified. There are many times when I reflect during this stage, and although I struggle, I would not change a thing because it is part of the defining mystique that encompasses me.

"The most pathetic person in the world is someone who has sight, but has no vision."
—Helen Keller

The certification stage creates a sense of satisfaction that affirms that one is tried, true, and proven with the spirit of perseverance as one's guide and comforter. In this stage, one weathers the storm and holds firm in one's faith and beliefs; one begins to experience the moment of clarity that embraces the soul and rewards the heart with inner peace. There is no greater feeling than the sense of accomplishment when one begins to bask in the glow of the newfound sense of accomplishment.

When the resonating glow rests, one has entered the elevation stage. One finds favor in all that one does. This stage is truly an amazing time that many seek but fall short—the requirements of Trio interact and make no apology for the bountiful rewards.

When a person has truly tapped into its power, vision plays heavily on that person's emotions. It gives the opportunity to see him- or herself in a role that is in agreement with that person's true character and defined purpose; it can also show alignment with what he or she is meant to be—this is when true vision has been realized.

In addition, vision allows a person to take inventory and assess the multiple opportunities that have been taken advantage of or left behind. The vision is real because an individual can see it before it actually happens. Vision is extremely powerful (Jones, Interview)!

In *10 Passions of a Man's Soul: Harness Your Strength, Impact Your World*, Mark Elfstrand chronicles the purpose of today's male by diving into the essence of vision where men are concerned. He states, "Today we see a disturbing lack of understanding about real manhood. One reason is a lack of good role models. We also suffer from a lack of vision as to what a man is and how he should act."

The ten passions of men are Purpose, Adventure, Power, Winning, Wealth, Self-Preservation, The Hunt, Pleasure, Relationships, and Legacy. The author breaks them into smaller components.

Purpose has four elements: Ambition (which must be tempered by self-control); Duty (which must be connected to honor), Calling (which is best when directed by God), and Cause (which must be worth pursuing).

Adventure is composed of the Unknown, the Thrill, the Risk, and Living Dangerously. "You will not experience the depth of your manhood until you experiment with adventure; but choose wisdom over foolishness in making decisions."

The components of the Passion for Power are strength, intimidation, leadership, control, and domination. You can use these elements selfishly or for a higher good. Remember that there is power in humility.

The Passion for Winning needs an opponent, a game plan, an engagement, a crisis point, and a reward. Competition is healthy, but we must play fair and play to win. Losing is temporary; building each other up is everlasting because life is a team sport.

The Passion for Wealth includes accumulation, spending nature, quality preference, stewardship, and philanthropy. The Passion for Self-Preservation is made up of basic needs, identity, emotional survival, and protected care.

The Passion for the Hunt needs the assignment, the provision, the calling, the mastery, and the challenge of keeping perspective. The Passion of Pleasure involves biological response, satisfaction quotient, contrasts, and consequences. "God wants us to celebrate life—but always within His design."

The Passion of Relationships is composed of the relational levels, priorities, fundamentals, and risks. The Passion of Legacy requires a purpose statement, set of values, and impact criteria.

The essence of a man's vision is tied into his ability to see himself in his core element, at his highest potential, walking out his purpose, and living his passion. Only then will he have become the true leader he was meant to be and exist in the reality of his own vision.

"Leadership is the capacity to translate vision into reality." —Warren Bennis

We are all leaders in our sphere of influence. In all that we do, we must see ourselves in the moment of achievement through visualization. What we see, believe, and confess, will ultimately manifest.

Notes

Notes

Notes

Notes

What is **Versatility** in the Trio

Chapter 3

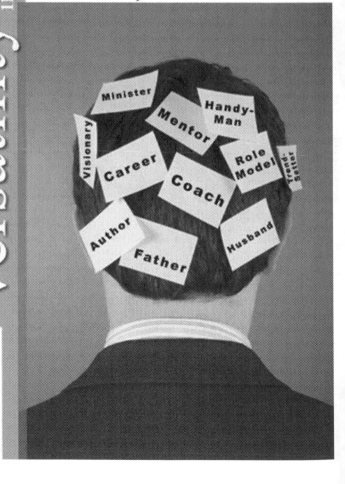

Minister

Visionary

Mentor

Handy-Man

Career

Role Model

Coach

Trend-Setter

Author

Father

Husband

Chapter 3

Versatility in the Trio

Versatility is adaptability, flexibility, resourcefulness, usefulness, and changeability. It means that one is capable of easily adapting to various tasks, fields of endeavor, etc; it also means having or being capable of many uses.

In *To Survive in This Job Market, Be Versatile and Flexible*, Tony Rogers explains, "Your dream job may be one you never dreamed you'd be doing."

Even though the article is to journalists about journalism, his article explains the importance of versatility and flexibility. The principles behind versatility remain the same—regardless of the intended vocation. The article explains that, in today's society, you must be armed with as many skills as possible in your craft. In essence, if you are a journalist, you should not limit your skill set to writing. You should learn the technological areas of your craft to stay competitive in the marketplace. In other words, you must be versatile in the workplace.

One major way to become and remain versatile is to always continue educating yourself in the latest advancements of your profession.

According to Michael Leimbach, PhD, versatility is based upon the Wilson Learning Social Style model. Nearly half a century of research proved that people are divided equally across four primary communication styles. These four social styles are: Driver, Expressive, Amiable, and Analytical. When a person is easy to communicate or work with, it is often because you share the same social style. When a person seems difficult to work with, it is often because your styles are different. Versatility skills allow you to effectively and pleasantly communicate with people of all social styles.

For example, in *The Guide for Personal Growth*, the article titled "The Importance of Being Flexible" states, "Being flexible and versatile is an advantage if you have the desire to succeed at anything you do. You will experience day-to-day difficulties, delays and frustrations in your demanding work, life, and when dealing with people. There are even times when you have to deal with situations that do not fit in or interrupt your schedules."

Versatile individuals adapt quickly to unexpected changes; they are flexible and resilient, fitting easily and comfortably into any situation.

Versatility is the core essence to our internal light. Our core essence is best described as the nucleus that, when utilized, serves as a continuous surge to greatness. The presence of this light captures our deepest fears and hidden emotions, and it utilizes them as inspiration to motivate our true underlying purpose. Many of us are held captive by the inability to understand the significance of the strategically aligned power in our element of directional change. A lack of understanding sudden changes causes stagnation; one should adjust quickly, aligning with the powers or authority that be, submit, and then work within that scope—flexibility is the key. In this regard, you make yourself as agile and versatile as the fox.

Versatility is a plus for the fox because it can easily live in the sweltering Sahara Desert or in icy regions of

Europe, Asia, and North America. It can adjust its diet from eating roadkill to eating fruit. To be versatile is to adapt to different environments, careers, people, or circumstances without a whimper. To be versatile is to make the best of a bad situation. Versatility is the final part of the dynamic Trio.

Steps to Becoming More Versatile:

Step 1: Build stronger relationships by valuing yourself and others.

Step 2: Focus on relational needs. Learn how to communicate in the following:

- How to convince

- How to motivate

- How to tactfully disagree

Step 3: Develop positive attitudes.

Step 4: Identify tension areas in your behavior that may cause tension to yourself and others. Alleviate them.

Step 5: Take steps to improve personal and professional skills and relationships. Learn more about your current occupation or, better yet, learn to branch out into new areas of it. When you allow yourself to become more versatile, you will have completed the Trio—values, vision and versatility—and the full reality of greatness will be at your fingertips.

Notes

Notes

Notes

Notes

Chapter 4

Words of Wisdom

Chapter 4

Words of Wisdom

"In life, there is no such thing as coincidence; the things we encounter or accomplish over a period of time do not happen by osmosis. Each of us has a defined purpose that, at some point in time, will manifest and uncover unanswered questions that can suppress our joy. In all that one does, let love be the captain that navigates one's purpose to impact, inspire, and energize the will of others."

"Circumstances, situations, obstacles, strongholds, recessions, and setbacks are powerless words that scour the mind until spoken into existence. We are heirs and coheirs to the kingdom of Heaven, and we choose not to accept anything less than the promise of our inheritance."

"Foundational life-building blocks are only as good as the personal influences that establish a solid core substance. Each layer of substance uncovers depth through knowledge and understanding. In all that we do, the passion for understanding and clarity must remain paramount."

"There are many times when failure is excusable, but not trying because of the possibility of failure leaves no excuse at all. In everything one does, there are endless possibilities for those who are willing to try—especially those who are stifled by disappointment."

"Visual manifestation is the ability to subconsciously engage in the anticipated moment of success, which ultimately leads to an overflow of benevolence. In everything you do, remember to spiritually release the unimaginable power of supernatural favor through the power of positive thinking."

"Decisions are internal vessels that lead to crossroads. Each crossroad is surrounded by thoughts of analytical and strategic knowledge that takes a second—if absorbed—to impact our lives. The meaningful decisions one allows to manifest will impact one's happiness for a lifetime."

"The quest for success is like an adrenaline junkie on an endless thrill, forever searching for more. This thrill is like none other and, when experienced, fills even the deepest voids with the echoing sounds of accomplishments. Timeless thrills can be experienced, in all that one does, through the interlocking actions of hard work and determination."

"There are many melodies in the world, but what makes each unique? There are many phrases and quotes, but what captivates one's attention? Each day, we have a unique opportunity to be the exception. Will you become the song that's consistently requested, the cliché of all quotes, or the commanding presence? Start today by solidifying your existence as a necessity."

"Commitment is the cornerstone that consistently identifies and establishes the foundational roots of a champion. The hallmark of validity is consistent reproducible results. In all that one does, let one's actions lead by example and serve as a direct correlation to one's everyday words."

"There are three essential qualities that are required in everyday life: life, laughter, and love. Life gives us a sense of being, laughter releases and rewards the heart with joy, and love gives us a compassionate heart to serve and reward others. Remember to take a moment each day to enjoy the pure bliss that each of the three essentials provides."

"Success is a probability of faith; it is a result of diligent work and determination. Individuals who use it as a tool for measurement frequently find disappointment. No instrument can measure the success of a single individual when we strive to make those around us better."

"Opportunity seeks those who strategically prepare for the moment of expectation. When preparation is solidified, desires of the heart are fulfilled—and each challenging task is successfully accomplished. Opportunity finds those who have successfully prepared for its arrival."

"We work to live instead of live to work. Each day should be meaningful and have a true defined purpose. In everything one does, make sure that passion and desire consistently serve as majority stakeholders."

"A simple smile serves as an emotional gateway to the heart. It pierces the toughest regions of unexplored compassion and leads to joyful bliss. Despite the challenges one may face, always remember to start the day off with a smile."

"The true test of a champion is one that allows misfortunes or setbacks to serve as mental stimulation. These activated sensors trigger an inner winning desire that can only be unleashed when the term "impossible" is nonexistent. In all that one does, know that greatness is one's path, which activates one's inner beacon of light."

"Time is consistently mismanaged and is seldom cherished. Take a moment to pause and appreciate the key essential element that most take for granted."

"At times, the inevitable appears to be the norm. It's amazing how word placement plays a significant role in the final outcome of everything. Remember to speak into existence our desires and needs!"

"Hope gives way to dreams, which is the first step in the visualization process. Before an individual can accomplish any feat, he or she must have a desire that has been brought about through faith. Hope never fails us;

a lack of desire sometimes takes away from our dreams and desires. Dream big!"

"Solidify oneself as a presence and not a mere mist. A mist lasts only a second, but a powerful presence is remembered for a lifetime."

"Life gives reflection to the multiple footprints we have established in search of a greater understanding of our ultimate purpose. Some footprints are deeper than others—as a result of the positive or negative lessons learned. Our ultimate goal is for one deserving individual to bear the hope-filled reflection of the seed we plant."

"When hatred and malice are manifested, they spiritually disable our ability to tap into the abundant land of harvest. We often miss supernatural appointments and blessings because we harbor hatred or are unwilling to forgive one another. Joy and evil cannot dwell in the same body; choose which master you wish to serve."

"At times, there is a misunderstanding between empathy and sympathy. Many of us apply them to various situations in our daily lives. Empathy brings about an understanding, whereas sympathy provokes heartfelt thought that shows compassion. Change can only occur when compassion is present in the heart; it tears down the prideful walls of resistance."

"Understanding sheds light on past experiences through upbringing and personal exposure. Many of us are misunderstood due to a lack of desire to enlighten ourselves, which makes room for personal and cultural differences. Knowledge gives birth to the suppressed world of acceptance. Challenge those around you to explore the brilliant possibilities of the wonderful world of change."

"If giving were the reason to live, some of us would be dead. How often does one give love, time, or financial support to those in need? Our existence is to serve, which triggers conviction as a result of past experiences."

"Successful individuals are rarely failures, and failures find it difficult to succeed. The two are subconsciously connected and are only separated by small decisions. The choice is ultimately up to you. We can't be pitiful and powerful in the same body. Choose one."

"Would-have, could-have, and should-have individuals are always a day late and a dollar short. Where do you fit into the equation of making things happen instead of having nothing more than agreed-upon potential?"

"What is your legacy, and how much of an impact have you had on the world? Are you living to work or working to live? The true answer can be found within one's internal peace—and this can only be experienced once one has discovered one's true passion."

"The path to greatness takes more than spoken words to appease the unequally yoked naysayers. It's a calculated expression that must be born in the spirit in order for the transformation to naturally occur."

"Synergistically connect yourself to a solid foundational establishment that truly exemplifies the worth of example. The connection one establishes is the key to unlocking one's chamber of hidden treasures."

"Greatness is not defined by the amount of accolades and accomplishments one has achieved—but by the amount of lives one touches through kind gestures, selfless acts, and a servant's heart of humility. The greatest gift one could ever give is the gift of time. Remember to share your gift with someone today; the impact will last a lifetime."

Notes

Notes

Notes

Notes

Notes

Ponder This...

Chapter 5

Chapter 5

Ponder This

New Shoes

All new shoes hurt if you wear them long enough. Please don't get misled; just because something is new doesn't make it better. Many times, you haven't had a chance for the imperfections or flaws to discover your areas of discomfort, which brings a false sense of satisfaction.

The Competitor and the Entertainer

In life, there are competitors and entertainers. Competitors rise to the level of competition, and entertainers go through life and serve as the joke, constantly amusing the world. You can be the exception and exemplify both as a competitor who entertains with unique talents and abilities, hard work, and labor.

The Smart Investor

The smart investor is one who accesses his or her talents and abilities while planning for the future and strategically aligning activities with what will give the best chance for future opportunities. As smart investors are beginning to invest time into each stock, they are making sure that all time and efforts are geared toward the most aggressive return on investment.

Unpredictable Attraction

In life, most men and women are fascinated by mental stimulation. Both sides prefer a sense of suspense and controlled unpredictability that maintains excitement in a relationship. The Rubik's cube was the top-selling gadget in the 1980s, but it fell to the wayside after losing its element of suspense and being figured out. As long as there is suspense and controlled unpredictability, passion and excitement will follow.

Quantum Leap Theory

We are often placed in situations for a much bigger cause than we understand, and many times we stay in a holding pattern or stalemate until we accomplish our task or mission.

The understanding isn't always clear at the time, but your soul will be at peace once the moment of clarity arrives.

The Will to Succeed

This internal drive is the foundation of determination; it is based upon the premise of mental desire. Success starts with a calculated emotional expression that is brought forth through visual expectation. Through faith, this command materializes in the spirit that exposes the passion expressed in the heart.

A man's desires are exposed through the heart, and the spirit sends signals to those who share the same vision.

The Lazy Carpenter

The lazy carpenter works sporadically for years to build a home. As he gets closer to the completion of his dream, he becomes more complacent and inconsistent due to his inability to focus on the task at hand. As many begin to look on in amazement while admiring his work, he gives a fellow carpenter the final task to complete it. The second carpenter takes the credit for all of his work. Remember to finish what you start and end all tasks with the same enthusiasm as you began with.

No

Never be afraid to ask for the things you truly desire—as long as you use them to inspire others. "No" has never caused an individual to fall dead; until "no" starts killing, do not stop asking for what is wanted or needed. Part of understanding a true need is to effectively learn how to express and communicate it to another.

Excuses

"Excuses are tools of incompetence that are used to build monuments of nothingness. They are signs of weakness and symbols of ignorance and those who use them will never fulfill their dreams."
—Anonymous

Notes

Notes

Notes

Notes

Bibliography

Elfstrand, Mark. *10 Passions of a Man's Soul: Harness Your Strength, Impact Your World.* Chicago, IL: Moody Press, 2006.

Jones, Edna., ed. *Values, Vision, Versatility: The True Power of the Trio*, Coral Springs, FL: 2012.

Leimbach, Michael, PhD, Wilson Learning Worldwide. Edina, MN: 2012.

McLaughlin, Corrine. *Soul Light: Science of the Soul.* 2002. Center for Visionary Leadership. March 3, 2012.

http://www.visionarylead.org/aboutus.htm
© 2002 by Corinne McLaughlin

Orans, Lewis P. "What are Values?" The Pine Tree Web, 1996.

Posner, Roy. "The Power of Personal Values." Growth Online, 2008.

About the Author

Corey Hicks is truly an inspirational humanitarian who was brought up from humble beginnings and raised in Chattanooga, Tenn. While growing in the inner city he encountered several obstacles and temptations that served as life lessons and inspiration to persevere.

Through hard work and determination, Mr. Hicks attended Kentucky State University where he received a B.A. Degree in Early Childhood Education while excelling in the Decathlon as a two-time NCAA All-American. After graduation, he placed his career on hold while his talents granted him the opportunity to train in San Louis Obispo, CA with one of the premier coaches of Track and Field, Coach Brooks Johnson as part of the 1996 Olympic Hopeful Team.

He trained among many of the greats and was destined for stardom until an untimely injury occurred just before the Olympics that temporarily derailed his dream to compete.

After being given the news that his injury would be a major setback, and he would have to wait another four years to fulfill his dream, he then begins to utilize his experiences as a teaching tool to encourage, motivate and inspire. Mr. Hicks currently hold a Masters Degree in Health Science and is completing his Ph.D. in Health and Human Performance.

Mr. Hicks has been a motivational speaker for over 21 years and has successfully spoken both nationally and internationally. Mr. Hicks has presented for the Caribbean Sports Ministries, as well as major corporations within the U.S. He currently serves as a successful Sr. level Sales Representative within the Biotech Industry, and is also the founder and CEO of the Three V's Foundation.

The concepts expounded in his book Values, Vision, and Versatility has truly played a significant role in the guidance and transformation of what he was to become and who he is today. He is a living example of the phrase "All things are possible".